PET OWNER'S GUIDE TO THE
WHIPPET

Anne Vickerstaff

RINGPRESS

ABOUT THE AUTHOR

Anne Vickerstaff has been involved with Whippets for nearly 30 years. She established her kennel of Rystone Whippets in 1973 and established a reputation for breeding sound, quality dogs. She has enjoyed considerable success in the show ring and also judges the breed.

Anne is a member of the Whippet Club, and is honorary secretary of the South West Whippet Club. She has recently started racing her Whippets, which she – and her dogs – enjoy immensely.

Published by Ringpress Books,
A Division of INTERPET PUBLISHING
Vincent Lane, Dorking, Surrey RH4 3YX

First published 2002
©2002 Ringpress Books. All rights reserved

Design: Rob Benson

ISBN 1 86054 188 7

Printed and bound in Hong Kong through Printworks International Ltd.

CONTENTS

CARING FOR THE ADULT WHIPPET

Feeding; Grooming; Exercise; The rescued Whippet; Caring for the oldies; Euthanasia.

THE VERSATILE WHIPPET

Racing (Getting started; Time to compete); Lure coursing; Coursing; Agility; Competitive Obedience; The show dog (Is my dog good enough?; Getting started; At the show).

HEALTH CARE

Preventative care (Internal parasites; External parasites; Vaccinations); A-Z of common ailments (Alopecia; Anaesthetics; Anal glands; Constipation; Cystitis; Diarrhoea; Ear infections; Epilepsy; Gastric torsion; Heat stroke; Infectious diseases; Pyometra; Rhinitis; Skin conditions; Undescended testicles; Vomiting; Summary.

1

Introducing The Whippet

The Whippet is one of the most popular members of the Hound Group. A versatile dog, with an even disposition, the Whippet was bred to run at speed over short distances. Today, the Whippet is still used for racing, but his outstanding role is as an affectionate and intelligent companion that enjoys the company of his owners and of other Whippets.

TRACING ORIGINS

The Whippet is depicted in many works of art; small dogs of Greyhound type can be found in paintings and sculptures from as early as the 6th century BC.

There are many theories as to how the Whippet evolved as a breed. There are obviously strong links with the Greyhound as Whippets are, after all, Greyhounds in miniature. Another line of thought is that they were bred by miners in the north-east of England specifically for racing. In this part of the world, they were known as snap dogs. There are claims that the Whippet was developed by crossing the Manchester Terrier, the Old English White Terrier, and the Italian Greyhound. The aim was to create a dog with a terrier's gameness and tenacity, combined with the speed, stamina and grace of a Greyhound.

My personal belief is that there has always been a small Greyhound-like dog that was used for coursing small game like rabbits, and, later, for the popular sport of racing.

Going back to the early domestication of the dog, there is no doubt that dogs of Greyhound type have best preserved the characteristics of their ancestors. The elongated lines, narrow head, pointed nose which overshoots the mouth, thin lips, and small ears lying close to the head are typical

Left: The Whippet has strong links with the Greyhound.

Right: The Italian Greyhound may have been used in developing the Whippet breed.

of many of the sighthounds. The chest is usually deep and fairly narrow but with plenty of heart room, the stomach is tucked up, the bones are long and flat, the muscles are well developed and very visible. The size of the game to be hunted determined the size of hound developed by man to perform the task. The Borzoi was bred to hunt wolf, whereas the smaller Greyhound/Whippet was used to hunt rabbit, hare and smaller ground game.

Interestingly, there are records of broken- or rough-coated Whippets. Some believe that the curly-coated Bedlington Terrier, which is very similar in shape to the Whippet, may have been used to create the Whippet.

Personally, I rather think it may be the other way round – but, like many aspects of breed history, we have no concrete evidence for either theory, and are forced to rely on anecdote, speculation, and personal opinion.

Pioneers of the breed established a sound foundation of bloodlines.

FORMAL RECOGNITION

Whippets were first officially recognised by the Kennel Club in 1890. The Whippet Club, the oldest of the breed clubs, was formed in 1899 by a small but devoted group of Whippet fanciers. Breed pioneers, such as H. Bottomley (Shirley) and A. Lamotte (Manorley), were highly influential in creating the modern Whippet, and their kennel names (prefixes) are behind most Whippets today. We think of them as part of the history of the Whippet.

STALWARTS OF THE BREED

A number of breeders have made their names by breeding top-quality Whippets, and it is the stock they have produced that ensures the future health and wellbeing of the breed.

The famous Laguna Whippets, bred by the late Dorrit McKay, are known worldwide. Her daughter, L. Bond-Gunning, still holds the Laguna affix, and breeds Whippets for coursing and for the show ring.

The Shalfleet affix is owned by Barbara Wilton-Clark, a very talented breeder of Greyhounds and Whippets. The Shalfleet kennel produced a grand total of 19 English Champions, and many of today's Whippets have Laguna and Shalfleet in their pedigrees.

The Dondelayo kennel belongs to Anne Knight, and her beautiful bitch Ch. Dondelayo Duette made breed history by becoming the first Whippet to win the

Top-quality British Whippets were exported to the USA.

Hound Group and Reserve Best in Show at Crufts.

There are many other breeders who have been influential in the breed, and there is no doubt that their care in the past has given us the Whippet we know and love today.

THE WHIPPET IN AMERICA

The breed was first registered in America in 1888, two years before its official recognition in the UK. Whippet racing was the major interest at the time, as it was in the UK, and showing became more popular over the years.

The first male Whippet Champion in America was made up in 1903. He came from Bay View kennel, and was called Bay View Pride. There is no record of his colour. The first bitch Champion, a fawn, was owned by the Newton Abbot variety kennels, and she won her title a few months later. At that time, fawn was the most common colour; only one of the early Champions was black. In 1924, the breed received wider recognition when Best in Show at the Rochester show in New York went to an imported bitch, Ch. Towyside Teasle.

Throughout the history of the breed, there has been a constant flow of Whippets making the journey from the UK to the USA. In the 1930s, the Tiptrees kennel, owned by Stanley Wilkin, made a big contribution, followed by imports from Laguna, Dondelayo, Oldown, Seagift, Fleeting,Tantivvey, Flarepath, Greenbrae, Selbrook, and Charmoll.

Despite the British influence, the breed has developed along different lines in the USA. Whippets tend to be taller than most British dogs. They are more brightly coloured, longer in the neck, and higher on the leg. Judges who travel overseas need to be aware of this difference in type.

A blend of speed and stamina makes the Whippet an ideal racing dog.

OLD-STYLE RACING

Before the First World War, Whippet racing was a very popular sport. It spread from the north of England, which was its original home, to the south. In most places, Sunday was the traditional day for racing – except in Scotland where they raced on Saturday.

The Portobello Ground, in Edinburgh, was one of the best in the United Kingdom. Students from the university and many ladies entered their dogs to compete with those trained by the miners of the Lothian district. Many exciting races took place and considerable sums of money changed hands.

Whippet races were run on the flat, on a cinder or brick-dust track, 200 yards in length. They were run in heats of six or seven dogs, and each dog was distinguished by wearing a racing collar: red, white, blue, yellow, green or black. The dogs were handicapped by weight – the heavier the dog, the greater the handicap. The dogs were weighed before each race and kept in the paddock until it was time for the race. Then, each dog was taken to its handicap mark by the slipper.

At the sound of the starting pistol, the slippers would release the dogs. It was said that a good slipper could literally throw a dog into its stride, thus influencing

If mutual respect is established, a Whippet will get on well with children.

how his charge would run. The dogs would then race up the track to a 'rag', which was waved before them by their runners-up. A flag, showing the colour of the winning dog's collar, was then hoisted up on a pole for all to see.

The scenes at a big meeting must have been very exciting. The heats were run in swift succession, amid the noise of excited barking, the shouts of the runners calling to their dogs, the calls of the bookmakers, and the roar of the crowd. Things are very different today. Whippet racing is an amateur sport, so no money is involved. The dogs, who run for trophies, are started from traps, and so the slipper's role is lost. However, the sport still attracts many enthusiasts (see Chapter Six), and there is certainly no finer sight than that of a Whippet running at full speed.

THE COMPANION WHIPPET

The Whippet has a sweet nature,

and makes a perfect house dog. Like many hounds, the Whippet is fastidious about keeping himself clean, and his short coat is easy to groom.

The Whippet is friendly towards people and other dogs. This is an intelligent and sensitive breed that thrives on companionship. Children are readily accepted, as most Whippets love playing with a ball or knotted rope. The bonus is that the Whippet is not big or powerful, so small children can play with this breed without the risk of being knocked over. Whippets do not bark readily, but a self-respecting house dog will let you know if there are strangers about.

The Whippet is very keen on his creature comforts; he needs warmth and comfort, a bed out of draughts, or, preferably, your bed if that is allowed. Most Whippets spend a lot of time snoozing. They are not demanding about how much exercise they get, but most will appreciate the opportunity for a free run. However, the Whippet is a fair-weather friend. If it is raining, Whippets prefer to stay indoors. They hate getting wet and persuading them to go out when it is wet is not easy.

The Whippet is not the easiest dog to train. Most are very intelligent and quick to learn, but there is often a stubborn streak. Most Whippet owners share a sense of humour – which is essential when your Whippet takes the law into his own paws!

2 Choosing A Whippet

The decision to take on a Whippet – or a dog of any breed – must be regarded as a long-term commitment. Whippets can live for up to 15 years, some even longer. Are you prepared to take on the responsibility of caring for a dog for this period of time.

Whippets like companionship, and do not thrive if left alone for hours at a time. I would not allow one of my puppies to go to a home where the owners would be out all day, and I am sure other Whippet breeders would feel the same.

You must also consider the financial aspect. Whippets are not expensive to feed, but can you afford veterinary fees, or pay for boarding kennels if you go away on holiday?

Have you the time to devote to rearing and training a Whippet? Will your family commitments allow this?

If you have owned a Whippet before, you will know how they worm their way into your life. This is a very special breed that needs lots of affection. This is no hardship for the owner – and the love you give is returned in abundance.

If you, and your family, have decided that you are ready to take on a dog, and that a Whippet is the right breed, you should now start looking for a breeder.

FINDING A BREEDER

The first step is to contact your national Kennel Club, and ask for details of breed clubs. A breed club secretary will let you know if there are any shows you can go to, and will give you details of Whippet breeders in your area.

It is a good idea to visit a dog show or two, and have a good look at the Whippets on show. This will give you the opportunity to find out what colour and type you like. Whippets can be any

If you go to a show, you will be able to see different types of Whippet, and the full range of colours.

colour, or mixture of colours, so there is plenty to choose from. A Championship show will generally have over 100 Whippets for you to look at.

When you have been to a few shows and read all you can about the breed, you can start looking for the breeders who have the type of Whippet you would like. It is worth visiting a few breeders or Whippet owners to see the dogs in their home environment. A responsible Whippet owner/breeder would welcome your visit. I am always glad if people want to come and see my Whippets – and they love visitors!

VIEWING A LITTER

When you find a litter, make a list of questions you would like to ask; it is easy to forget matters of importance with the thrill of seeing puppies for the first time. You must also be prepared to answer all sorts of questions regarding your home, your children, your lifestyle, and the arrangements you will be making to accommodate a puppy. Many breeders will not let a puppy go if it is going to be kept in a kennel.

It is important to see the whole litter, with their mother (dam), so that you can get a good idea of temperament. The sire (the

It is important to see the mother with her pups to get an idea of temperament.

puppy's father) may not be available to view. In many cases, the sire will belong to another kennel, but it should be possible to see a photo.

The breeder may be planning to keep a puppy as a show prospect, so you may have to wait before you can make your own choice. Be patient, a good puppy is worth waiting for. Make sure you remember the following golden rules.

- Never buy a Whippet puppy from a third party, i.e. someone who is acting on behalf of the breeder.

- Always see the puppy with his mother or littermates, at the address where they were bred.
- Do not buy from a pet shop because you feel sorry for the puppy. You do not know the pup's history or his breeding – and you may not even end up with a purebred Whippet.

DOG OR BITCH ?

Most new owners seem to want a bitch, but if you are going to have only one Whippet, either male or female will make a good companion. A male puppy is more suitable for a family home, as you do not have to cope with a bitch's

Both male and female are equally loving and affectionate.

seasonal cycle. If you later decide to add another Whippet to your collection, wait until your first dog is around nine months of age, and then look for a male companion for him.

It is not a good idea to buy two pups from the same litter. You will find that the puppies are so focused on each other that they pay little attention to you. This is unrewarding, and also makes training very difficult.

A bitch has seasons, or comes on 'heat', about every six months. You have to keep a close watch on her and keep her away from all male dogs for the three weeks of her heat. This can be a nuisance, as she will attract male dogs nearby. You cannot keep an in-season bitch in the same house as a male that has not been neutered. This is unfair on both dogs, and could well result in serious behavioural problems.

If you have no plans to breed from your Whippet, it is a good idea to consider neutering. Your vet will help you to decide what is the best age to have this done. Generally, a bitch is spayed after her first season, and a male will be castrated at around eight or nine months.

If you choose a bitch puppy, please do not be tempted to have a litter because someone has told you it is good for a bitch to have one litter. There are enough puppies around that are not wanted, so do not add to them. A bitch will be quite happy without having puppies.

The puppies should be outgoing and friendly.

ASSESSING THE LITTER

The vast majority of responsible breeders will not allow you to see the puppies until they are about four weeks old, and up on their feet. The dam should look healthy, if a little wary, as she has her babies to protect. The puppies should be starting on solid food, to wean them off the dam.

Look for the following signs which indicate a well-reared litter:

- Puppies' accomodation should be clean and sweet-smelling.
- There should be room for the pups to play.
- They should look clean and healthy.
- They should be well covered rather than fat.
- Their eyes should be bright and sparkling.

- There should be no evidence of discharge from either the nose or the eyes.
- The nails should be clipped. (A puppy's nails must be trimmed regularly while he is still feeding from his mother, or he could scratch and hurt her).
- The pups should be reasonably outgoing at four weeks, and they should be interested in coming up to play with you.

Do not worry if the pups look more like baby Labradors than Whippets. Within a couple of weeks they will become finer and look more Whippet-like.

By six weeks of age, it is easier to make a choice, as the puppies will have started to emerge as individual personalities. The breeder will have spent a lot of

Often a puppy stands out in a litter, as if he is saying "Pick me!"

time watching the litter, and will be able to help you select a pup who is most likely to fit in with your lifestyle.

Do not expect to take your chosen puppy home until he is eight to ten weeks old; some breeders will not let puppies go to their new homes until they are twelve weeks old.

However, you can choose a name for your puppy, while you are waiting. The breeder can start calling your pup by name, and, when you are able to take your puppy home, he will know his name. This will help the little pup settle more easily.

SELECTING A SHOW DOG

If you decide you want a show dog, the process of choosing a pup is more complex. Generally, a person starts by buying a dog and then gets bitten by the 'showing' bug. In most cases, the next step is to go out and buy a pup that is worthy of showing.

If you are looking for a show prospect, go to as many shows as possible. Look carefully at the dogs being shown, and learn about the breeders whose stock you admire. Remember to think about temperament as well as appearance.

When you feel ready, approach

It is better to wait until a pup is a little older before selecting a show prospect.

the breeder of your choice and ask if it is possible to buy a puppy with show potential from them. Obviously, a breeder cannot guarantee that an eight-week-old puppy is going to become a Champion. It is best to wait until a pup is four to five months old. By that stage, you will have some idea of what you are buying.

Look for a balanced puppy, with good feet, strong bone, straight front legs, and strong hocks that do not turn in or out. The pup must catch your eye, and be bold. It is a good idea to take a friend who is experienced in the breed to help you assess conformation and temperament.

GETTING READY
Before you collect your puppy, you will need to visit a pet shop, and buy some basic equipment. If you can get to a Championship show, you can have a look at the trade stands, and you may well find that there are a number of special offers available.

BEDDING
Whippets like comfort and warmth, so your first purchase should be an easy-care fleece blanket. In fact, you should buy a couple, so that you always have a spare. These blankets are easy to wash, and tumble-dry very quickly. You can also buy doggy duvets

Whippets like their creature comforts, so a fleecy blanket should be one of your first purchases.

with removable covers for washing.

When the puppy is small, a big cardboard box makes a good bed. If it is chewed or soiled, you can simply dispose of it and get another. When your Whippet is bigger, it is worth buying a plastic, kidney-shaped bed. These are very cosy when they are lined with a blanket, and they are easy to keep clean.

Before your puppy arrives home, decide where he is going to sleep. You will need to find a quiet corner that is warm in the winter and cool in the summer. Most importantly, it must be free of draughts.

BOWLS

In the first few weeks, your pup will appreciate a small bowl (you can use a cat bowl) so that he can get at his food. When the pup is older, buy a stainless steel bowl. There are many types to choose from, including bowls with rubber feet to stop them slipping.

You will also need a bowl for drinking water, which should always be freely available. A heavy ceramic bowl, which cannot be tipped over, is a good choice.

CRATE

A dog crate to use as an indoor kennel, and for travelling, is invaluable. The puppy should

Make sure the toys you select are safe and will withstand chewing.

never be shut in the crate for long periods, but it can be used at times when the puppy cannot be supervised. It is also an aid to house-training (see Chapter Three).

The crate can be used in the car, which makes travelling a lot safer. It can also be used as an indoor kennel if you are staying away from home.

COLLAR AND LEAD

You will need to purchase a lightweight puppy collar. Most pet shops will stock the woven soft nylon type. It should not be too loose or the puppy will walk out of it, but it must accommodate the puppy's growth.

Buy a good-quality lead with a secure clasp. Some shops sell a puppy set which will last until your puppy is about five months old. Later, you will need to buy a suitable adult collar and lead.

Most Whippets wear wide collars, which come in a variety of designs. They may be decorated with studs, leatherwork images, or painted. You can also get leads to match.

ID

By law, all dogs have to wear a collar and identification disc which gives their owner's contact details. You may also consider a permanent form of ID, such as tattooing or microchipping. Ask your vet for advice.

TOYS

All puppies need toys to play with, particularly when they are teething. There is a huge variety available, so it is a matter of personal choice.

The safest toys to buy are cotton tug-toys or hard rubber toys, as these cannot be chewed into small pieces which could then be swallowed.

3 Caring For Your Puppy

At last the waiting is over, and it is time to collect your puppy. Try to arrange to collect your puppy as early as possible, as this will give him time to settle into his new home before nightfall.

If possible, take a friend to help you on the journey, while you concentrate on driving. You will need to be equipped with a towel, a blanket, and plenty of kitchen towels and wet wipes. Your puppy will not have been in a car before, and may well be car-sick. If you have a long journey, you should also take fresh drinking water.

Remember, your puppy will not have had his vaccinations, so try to avoid stopping. If you have to take a break, provide some newspaper if your pup needs to relieve himself, rather than letting him go on the ground. Most puppies are paper-trained and you should have no problem. The breeder will not feed a puppy prior to his journey, so, hopefully, your pup will settle to sleep in the car after a token protest.

PAPERWORK

Before you leave the breeder, make sure you have the following:

- A diet sheet, detailing the type of food your puppy has been fed on, when each meal is given, and how much he is given at each meal. The breeder will often let you have a little food for the first few days.
- The puppy's pedigree.
- Paperwork from the Kennel Club for transfer of ownership.

ARRIVING HOME

As soon as you get home, take your pup out into the garden to give him a chance to relieve himself. When he obliges, give lots of praise. You can then allow him to explore the garden. Some Whippet pups are very bold and

Give your puppy a chance to explore his new surroundings.

rush about in great excitement. Others are more cautious, and may slink along the ground, looking worried. Do not worry, just allow your pup to find his feet by giving encouragement but not making too much of a fuss.

Show your puppy where he is going to sleep. If you are using a crate, you can introduce your pup to it in easy stages. To begin with, leave the crate door open for the pup to go in and out as he pleases. When he has learnt that the crate is safe and comfortable, you can shut the puppy in for a few minutes at a time. When your puppy has accepted this, leave the room for a while so the puppy

gets used to being left on his own. A happy, confident puppy will soon learn that the crate is a cosy den, and will not fret if he is left for short periods.

MEETING THE FAMILY...

If you have children, they will be desperate to meet the arrival and want to start playing with him. Make sure you supervise introductions, and do not let the puppy become overwhelmed.

As I have mentioned earlier, Whippets are good with children. But is important that the pup is not regarded as a plaything. Children must be taught to respect the pup, and, equally, the puppy must learn to respect all members of his family – regardless of their age.

...AND OTHER ANIMALS

It is most important that you introduce your puppy to other pets you may own under careful supervision. The pup will soon learn who to respect, and who will play with him. If you already have a dog, make a fuss of him first before you fuss the puppy.

Cats can be difficult as they are unpredictable – though if your cat is used to dogs, you should have little trouble introducing your

If you already have a dog, supervise initial introductions and make sure the older dog does not feel left out.

Then give the two dogs a chance to make friends.

puppy into the household. An adult cat who is not used to puppies will prove more difficult, but, with time and patience, she will accept the newcomer. Do be careful; cats have sharp claws and move very quickly. Never leave your puppy alone with a cat until you are sure they get on together.

THE FIRST MEAL

You can offer your pup some food, and make sure he has a drink of fresh water. You may well find that your pup is more interested in exploring his surroundings than in eating. Do not worry – he will soon make up for lost time!

BEDTIME BLUES

The first night in a new home is stressful for puppy and owner alike. The puppy will miss the company of his littermates and will let his feelings be known.

The best course of action is to take your pup out to relieve himself, and then settle him in his crate. Some puppies seem to be reassured if a radio is left on low. Leave your pup without making a big fuss, and go to bed. It may help if you stay with your pup until he falls asleep, but, equally, your pup may refuse to settle if

To begin with, your puppy will miss the company of his littermates.

you stay with him.

It is inevitable that your puppy will cry, but, if he is in a crate, you know he cannot harm himself. Resist the temptation of taking your pup into bed with you – you will be starting bad habits which may prove very difficult to break.

FOOD AND FEEDING

To begin with, it is important to follow the breeder's feeding regime, using the same food, and feeding at roughly the same time. If your puppy's diet is changed, it will result in an upset stomach.

If you decide to change the diet after a couple of weeks, do so gradually over a period of a week. Mix a little of the food you intend to feed with the original food from the breeder until you are feeding your preferred food.

The puppy should be on four meals a day when he first arrives home. There are so many prepared foods available that feeding a balanced diet is easy. Do not be tempted to add vitamin supplements if you are using a complete puppy food, as it will upset the balance of the diet.

When your puppy is between three and four months of age, you will find he shows less interest in one of his meals – usually the early evening meal. The pup is ready to cut his food intake to three meals a day. If you like, you can feed a couple of dog biscuits in place of the meal until your puppy gets used to the change.

At six to seven months old, your puppy should be fed two meals a day. If you intend to feed once daily, you should start this when your Whippet is about twelve months old. In fact, a lot of people feed twice daily, and this seems to suit most Whippets. If you do feed once a day, give a snack as well, such as a couple of biscuits after a walk or at bedtime.

Do not change the diet or the feeding routine while your puppy is settling in.

Complete feeds are formulated to suit specific ages and lifestyles. To begin with, you will feed a puppy or junior diet. By the time your Whippet is 18-20 months old, he should be on an adult diet.

VACCINATION
All puppies should be vaccinated against distemper, hepatitis, leptospirosis, parvovirus and parainfluenza. Depending on where you live, your pup may also need to be vaccinated against rabies. Your puppy may have had his first vaccination before you take him home, so you must consult your vet and make arrangements to finish the course. If your pup is not been vaccinated, again, contact your vet as soon as possible to plan a suitable vaccination programme. This may vary depending on the vet's policy and the incidence of disease in your area.

After the initial vaccinations, your Whippet will need a booster injection once a year. If you have to board your Whippet in kennels, they will insist on proof of vaccination, and the same applies if you want to get involved with Whippet racing.

Keep an eye on your puppy after his vaccinations. Most dogs do not have an adverse reaction, but watch out for an upset stomach, or any other sign of ill health. If you are concerned, contact your vet immediately.

WORMING
The breeder of your puppy will have been worming the puppies since they were three weeks old, and you will need to follow the programme that has been recommended. If the puppy has not been wormed, contact your vet who will be able to give advice.

All puppies carry a burden of roundworm, and worming is essential for a young puppy to remain healthy.

HOUSE-TRAINING

Your puppy may have started learning to relieve himself outside before you take him home, or he may have been trained to use paper by the door. However, your puppy will be bewildered in his new home, so you will need to work on his house-training from scratch.

You will need to take your pup out at regular intervals:

- After every meal
- After a play session
- When he wakes from a sleep
- If you see your puppy sniffing or circling
- Every two hours (if he has not been taken out).

It is helpful if you go to the same spot in the garden, and use a command such as "Be Clean". In time, your pup will learn what is required. Always give lots of praise when your pup obliges, and have a game before you go back into the house.

The harder you work at house-training, the quicker your puppy will learn to be clean. Most dogs will not soil their sleeping quarters, and, if you are using a crate, this will aid the house-training process. At night, line the front half of the crate with paper, so your puppy does not soil his bedding. When he is a little older, he will be able to go through the night, waiting until he is let out in the morning before he relieves himself.

Never punish your puppy for making a 'mistake'. Nine times out of ten, it will be your fault for not reading the signs and taking him out.

EXERCISE

Do not be tempted to allow your puppy to have too much free running. Joints are very vulnerable while a pup is growing, and injury can result from too much exertion. Whippets are lively dogs and they love to race about, but it is essential to limit exercise during the growing period. When your Whippet is fully grown, you can take him for as many walks as you like.

DOS AND DON'TS

The Whippet is an easy breed to care for, but there are a few rules that should be observed:

DO NOT let your dog eat chicken bones or small cooked bones. Provide marrow-bones from the butcher if you can get them, or

It is essential to limit exercise while your puppy is growing.

smoked bones, roasted marrow-bones, or hide chews. If any sharp pieces break off, remove them quickly.

DO NOT allow your puppy free access to the garden unless you are confident that it has been puppy-proofed. This means ensuring that he cannot get at weedkillers or other chemicals. The garden must be securely fenced, and free from rubbish that could be harmful. A pup can get into trouble just by chewing pieces off an old plastic plant pot. If you use sprays in the garden, make sure they are not toxic to dogs.

DO NOT throw sticks for your puppy. A stick can easily get lodged across the roof of the mouth, or, worse still, it can puncture the throat. It is equally dangerous to throw stones for your puppy to fetch.

DO give your dog safe toys; a rope ragger is a great toy, and hard rubber rings or an empty cardboard box make fun things to play with.

DO NOT give your puppy old shoes to chew – he will not know that your new Gucci shoes are any different to your old slippers.

4 *Early Learning*

You are responsible for your puppy's all-round education, and this should start from the moment your puppy arrives home. Obviously, this does not mean embarking on lengthy training sessions, but it does mean establishing your role as leader so that your pup learns to accept your authority. It is essential that your puppy accepts his place in your family and does not seek to challenge it. A programme of kind but consistent training will result in a contented, well-behaved dog.

GIVING REWARDS

A dog will learn much more quickly if he is rewarded for his efforts. This can take many forms: you can give verbal praise, you can stroke or pat your dog, you can have a game with him, or you can give him a food treat. Find out what your puppy responds to, and then use this as a special reward when you are training.

Clicker training is becoming an increasingly popular method of training. Basically, a clicker is used to mark desirable behaviour, and then is followed up by giving a reward. The dog learns quickly and willingly, as he is being positively reinforced for correct behaviour. There are books available on clicker training, or you can find a training class that uses this system of learning.

Remember to keep training sessions short. A puppy has a limited concentration span, and will quickly lose interest. To begin with, a couple of minutes' training followed by a game will be ample. You can build up the sessions as your puppy matures, but the key is to make sure your Whippet is having fun, and is enjoying the time he is spending with you.

HOUSE RULES

Make sure your puppy knows the rules of the house from the

It is important for your Whippet to accept your leadership.

moment he arrives home, and make sure all members of the family apply them. If one person allows the puppy to jump up, and someone else tells him off for it, you will end up with a very confused individual.

All dog owners are different: some allow their dog to sleep on the sofa, others do not. It does not matter what you decide to do as long as you are consistent, and your Whippet knows what is expected of him.

I have found that "No", and "Off" are two very useful commands which can be used in a variety of situations.

If the puppy is chewing something you do not want destroyed, use a stern voice and say "No" very firmly. If the puppy carries on chewing, repeat the command. Make sure you do not confuse the pup by adding a stream of words, such as "No, you naughty, bad dog". Keep it simple, and your pup will be quick to learn.

The command "Off" can be used when your Whippet is in the wrong place. He could be

Use every opportunity to take your puppy out and about so that he can experience a variety of situations.

jumping up at you, trying to get on the sofa, or trampling over the flowerbeds. Get your puppy's attention by using his name, and then say "Off" very firmly, pointing to the ground. Remember to reward your pup as soon as he responds correctly.

"Leave" is another useful command, which has a variety of applications. You will discover that your Whippet is a curious dog, and loves to investigate everything he comes across. If he starts eating a nasty bit of rubbish, the "Leave" command is invaluable. It can also be used if you want your Whippet to give up the toy he is playing with.

To teach "Leave", place a biscuit on the floor and tell your dog to "Leave" when he goes towards it. Keep doing this, and he will soon learn. When the dog is successful and leaves the biscuit on the floor, you can use another command, such as "Okay", and allow him to take the reward.

SOCIALISATION

The aim of socialisation is to expose your puppy to as many different situations as possible so that he learns to be both well behaved and confident. He needs to get used to the sounds of traffic, walking among crowds in shopping centres, and meeting other animals.

If you have been working on your lead-training at home (see below), you should be ready to venture out when your puppy has completed his vaccinations. To begin with, your puppy will be distracted by all the new sounds and sights, and may forget his lead-training. Be patient, and encourage your puppy to walk with you, but be prepared for a few stops and starts during the first few outings.

Be prepared to work hard at this aspect of your puppy's training. Invent outings to go on, so that your puppy has every opportunity to learn about the ways of the world.

TRAINING CLUBS

Many veterinary practices run puppy socialisation parties which give the pups a chance to socialise with each other before they have completed their vaccination course.

When your puppy is fully vaccinated, it is important to find a training club.

This will enlarge your Whippet's experience of meeting dogs in a controlled situation, and you will also get help with training.

Make sure you choose a club that uses reward-based training methods. Ideally, the trainer will also have knowledge of the Whippet temperament.

BASIC EXERCISES

A Whippet puppy will learn quickly, and you can start work on basic exercises from an early age.

It is important to bear in mind that gentle persuasion and praise is the best way to teach your puppy. The Whippet is very sensitive, and will become worried and upset if he is shouted at.

Make training sessions fun, breaking up exercise with play.

LEAD-TRAINING

It may seem a tall order to start off by teaching lead-training. But it is an important prelude to teaching basic exercises, and being able to take your puppy out and about.

The first step is to get your puppy used to wearing a collar. If you have chosen a soft, lightweight collar, your puppy will not make too much of a fuss. Fit the collar and then distract your puppy with a game or a tasty treat. He may scratch at the collar to begin with, but he will soon forget that he is wearing it.

A Whippet may try to put on the brakes when he is first introduced to the lead.

With practice and praise, you will overcome initial reluctance and your Whippet will become a willing walking companion.

When your puppy is happy to wear his collar, you can attach a lead. Although you cannot take your puppy out until he has completed his vaccinations, you can use the time to practise walking on the lead. This can be done in the house, or in the garden.

Start by attaching the lead, and allowing it to trail as your puppy walks about. Make sure that the lead does not get tangled up. The next stage is to progress to holding one end of the lead, and following your puppy about.

When your puppy gets used to you holding the lead, you can encourage him to follow you. You can use a toy or a treat, and give lots of praise when your puppy walks with you.

The aim is to teach your puppy to walk on a loose lead, neither pulling ahead nor lagging behind.

This takes a fair amount of practice, so be prepared to reward a few steps of really good work, and then break off to have a game. If you progress in small stages, you are more likely to be successful.

The Stand is an essential exercise to learn for show dogs.

STAND

If you intend to show your Whippet, teach him the Stand position first; a sitting Whippet will not win prizes. Start by standing your puppy, and repeating the command "Stand". Praise your puppy and reward him when he stands for just a few seconds. You can gradually build up the time he stays in position.

When you feel confident that the puppy understands the command on the ground and on the table (in the show ring, a Whippet must stand on a table to be examined by the judge), you can proceed to the Sit position.

SIT

This exercise can be taught using a treat which you hold just above your puppy's head. As he looks up, he will naturally go into the Sit. If he shows any hesitation, you can apply gentle pressure on the hindquarters. As your puppy goes into the Sit, use the verbal command "Sit", so that your pup associates the command with the action. Give your puppy lots of praise when he is in the Sit position.

If a treat is held above your Whippet's head, he will naturally go into the Sit position.

DOWN

The next command is the Down. This is not an easy command, as the dog has to lie on the ground, and Whippets are fussy about where they lie.

Start with your Whippet in the Sit position, and kneel down or squat beside your puppy. Hold a treat just below your puppy's nose, and lower it to the ground.

Your Whippet will follow the lure, and will, hopefully, go into the Down position. Give the verbal command "Down" as your Whippet responds. This may take a little time, so reward any movement towards the Down position.

With some dogs, it may work better if you start from a Stand, and then lower the treat towards the ground. A slight pressure on the shoulder may encourage your Whippet to go into position. Give lots of praise, and then try the exercise again.

Once your Whippet has learnt this command, he can be left in the Down for a few seconds and you can extend the time he stays in position over a period of time.

STAY

By now, your Whippet is ready to learn the Stay command. Attach

The Down is a natural progression of the Sit exercise.

the lead, tell your Whippet to "Sit", and tack the word "Stay" after it, so you say "Sit-stay". Step a few paces back, holding the lead but not putting any tension on it.

If your Whippet tries to get up, return to his side and repeat the command calmly. This time, as you leave your Whippet, hold your right hand out, palm towards him. Once you can walk a lead's length away and your Whippet is staying in position, try the exercise off-lead. If your dog gets up, go back and firmly, but gently, take him back and repeat the command given. Always end a training session on a good note, with loads of praise as your Whippet completes the exercise.

Enjoy the time you spend training, and relations between dog and owner will certainly benefit.

COME

The next exercise is the most important of all – the Recall. To start with, you can do a few fun Recalls, using the command "Come", preceded by your Whippet's name. If he responds enthusiastically, you can try a more formal approach.

Put your dog in the Sit position, then walk away a short distance. Turn and face your dog, and say his name followed by the command "Come". If your dog hesitates, give lots of verbal encouragement. You can even try jumping up and down, or running for a few steps, so that you appear really exciting. When your Whippet responds, be lavish with your praise. In time, you can add a "Sit" as your dog comes in to you,

and then reward him with a treat.

The Whippet is a sighthound, and he has strong chasing and hunting instincts. In fact, some Whippets just cannot be trusted off the lead unless they are in a securely fenced field. Fortunately, this is not the norm – the vast majority of Whippets will come back when called.

If you do have a problem, try putting a long line on your Whippet's collar. Let him run off, and then call him back. If he ignores you, call again, this time giving a sharp tug on the line that will make him take notice. Call again. If he still disobeys, repeat the tug, calling him to come to you, pulling the line and drawing him towards you.

When your Whippet does eventually return, give him loads of praise – make him happy to come back. Keep trying and, hopefully, he will learn to come back when called. I know Whippets can be stubborn, so be gentle and firm. Never tell your dog off when he comes back to you (even though you may feel like it). That is the worst thing you can do. Always praise your dog for doing what you wish him to do – even if you have been standing in a field for an hour...

5 Caring For The Adult Whippet

The Whippet is an easy breed to care for, and if you follow the guidelines outlined below, you will encounter few problems.

FEEDING

I feed my adult Whippets twice a day. They have a complete feed, and I may add some green tripe, fish or meat to this. Complete feeds have all the vitamins and minerals your Whippet needs to stay healthy, so do not be tempted to add supplements such as calcium or vitamin pills, as it will upset the balance of your dog's diet. Make sure fresh water is always available, as some tend to

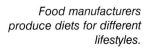

Food manufacturers produce diets for different lifestyles.

drink more when they are fed on a complete diet. You can, if you wish, pre-soak the food.

There are many complete feeds on the market; I have found that it pays to buy a good-quality one. Look at the contents on the bag, and try to buy one without artificial colours and additives if possible. Most of the diets are specially formulated to suit the age of the dog – puppy, junior, adult, and veteran for the older dog. Some dog food manufacturers also produce high-protein foods for working dogs and racing dogs.

Some owners find that canned food is a more convenient method of feeding. There is a huge variety of flavours and types, and most dogs eat this type of food with relish. Again, take the time to look at the label and find out the balance of nutrients. Some brands are better than others, and you need to avoid those with a high jelly content. Canned food should be fed with a wholemeal mixer.

Whippets will eat vegetables, cooked or raw. My dogs line up for a piece of carrot, a cabbage or cauliflower stalk, or the odd sprout. They also love cooked spring greens mixed with their food. Avoid giving cooked potatoes, as Whippets do not seem to be able to digest them very well. Rice and pasta go down well with a bit of cheese on top.

If you want to introduce variety into your Whippet's diet, try giving raw green tripe, ground beef, or cooked breast of lamb mixed with biscuit meal. If your dog is slightly off-colour, or getting on in years, cooked fish or chicken with rice is a good option.

The quantity you feed depends on your Whippet's size and appetite. The manufacturers give guidelines, but the best advice is to look at your Whippet and decide if you are feeding enough. You should be able to feed the same amount each day, and your Whippet should look healthy and well covered (not fat), and should maintain his weight.

GROOMING

The Whippet's smooth, fine coat is easy to care for. A daily grooming session with a bristle brush, plus a massage with a rubber hound glove, will keep the coat in order and the skin healthy.

Your puppy should be accustomed to standing on a table and being groomed from an early age. Some struggle a bit to begin with, but most learn to enjoy the attention.

The Whippet's short, fine coat is easy to care for.

A tooth scaler can be used to remove tartar from the teeth.

The nails should be checked, and trimmed when necessary.

NAILS

Nails should be checked weekly, and trimmed as required. You can buy nail-clippers specially for dogs, but I find the human nail-clippers work just as well. Make sure you only trim the tip of the nail, otherwise you will cut into the quick which will result in bleeding. After clipping, I use a file to smooth the rough edges. The pads should be checked for cuts and grazes, particularly after exercise.

DENTAL CARE

Your Whippet puppy will start teething at about four months old, and it is important to get your puppy used to having his mouth examined before this time.

When all the adult teeth are through, check them weekly for tartar, as some dogs seem more prone to it than others. You can buy a toothbrush and toothpaste specifically for dogs – follow the instructions and brush daily.

Hard biscuits and large marrow-bones will help to keep your Whippet's teeth in tip-top condition.

EYES AND EARS

I also check eyes and ears on a daily basis. The ears should look clean inside, with no evidence of a bad odour. If the ears look a bit mucky, get some cotton-wool (cotton), and wipe them gently. Do not attempt to probe into the ear – you will do more harm than good. Check the eyes, and, if necessary, wipe the corners gently with cotton-wool (cotton). If the eye appears inflamed, consult your vet.

EXERCISE

The first and most important aspect of exercise is to make sure you have a collar and lead that are safely and securely fitted, and that your dog has an identity disc. You will also need to be equipped so that you can clean up after your dog.

Road walking keeps the pads hard and the feet tight.

The adult Whippet benefits from a mixture of road walking and free-running. If a dog is exercised on different surfaces, it keeps the pads hard and the feet tight. The number of walks a day you provide is a matter of personal preference. Whippets are adaptable, and will fit in with your lifestyle. However, they love the opportunity to free-run. Whippets were bred to run, and it is a thrill to watch a dog using all his muscles, twisting and turning, and stretching out at full speed. If you have more than one Whippet, you will have great fun watching them chase each other. But if it is raining, you can forget it! You will find that your Whippet is loath to go out and will bury himself under his blankets.

If you are showing, racing or coursing, your Whippet will need more controlled exercise to keep him in hard condition. This may include road walking for a couple of miles every day, followed by a short blast off the lead. On returning home, the working dog will benefit from a massage.

THE RESCUED WHIPPET

If you decide you would like to take on an older or rescued Whippet, contact your local breed club secretary who will have contacts with Whippet rescue organisations.

The rescue organiser will contact a local home checker to visit your home and assess your suitability as a rescued Whippet owner. Your garden will have to be secure, and

A rehomed Whippet needs special understanding during the settling-in period.

arrangements must be made so that the dog is never left alone for longer than four hours a day maximum.

If you pass the interview and a Whippet becomes available, try to find out his history. A lot of older dogs end up in rescue because their owners cannot cope with them through family break-up, bereavement, or because they are moving abroad. However, in some cases, there may be behavioural problems, so it is important to find out why a Whippet is in rescue.

Sometimes, a breeder will run on two or three puppies from a litter, and then select one for showing. The other pups will be sold to pet homes, and this is an excellent option if you want a slightly older dog. It is worth contacting breeders to find out if any young adults are available.

If you know your Whippet's history, you should have little problem settling him in. Be patient, and give him time to become accustomed to his new life and the new people in his family. Do not be tempted to let a rescued Whippet off the lead until he is responding reliably to the Recall in the house and in the garden.

If you have no details of your Whippet's background, you may find that he takes a little longer to settle. For example, he might not have travelled in a car before, and may be worried by the new experience. He might have been with a lot of other Whippets and will feel lost without canine company. In some cases, a rehomed Whippet is very anxious and becomes upset when he is left.

The answer to most problems is to be patient and try to build up your Whippet's trust. In this situation, a crate is an invaluable aid, as it gives the Whippet a safe haven, and, if he is worried about being left, he cannot become destructive.

To begin with, spend as much time as you can with your Whippet, and build up the amount of time he spends in his crate in easy stages. It helps if you cover the top of the crate with bedding, as this makes it more like a den. Leave the door open, and you will find that your Whippet starts to go into his crate when he wants to rest.

Do not try to rush the settling-in period. A rescued Whippet is certain to feel bewildered and confused in the first few months, but, given time, he will learn to trust you and will become part of the family.

As your Whippet gets older, you will need to assess his changing needs.

CARING FOR THE OLDIES

Like old people, Whippets get slower as they get older. The trouble is, a Whippet is often a poor judge of his capabilities, and may become overtired by attempting to do too much. Some older dogs will be keen to go out for long walks, but not all. By the time your Whippet is around ten years old, start doing the thinking for him, and work out how much exercise is appropriate. I have a bitch who is nearly 14. She still plays like a puppy, but she will not go for a walk – she prefers to stay home.

The older Whippet should change to a lower-protein diet to help the kidneys function properly. Sometimes, an elderly Whippet may have dental problems, so a softer feeding regime should be adopted. It may help digestion if you feed three small meals a day.

Do not let your older Whippet get overweight. Keep a check on the quantity you are feeding as your dog becomes less active. It is not kind to overindulge your dog so that he becomes obese – it will only lead to an increase in health problems.

You may notice that your Whippet does not hear so well. This can lead to a potentially dangerous situation if your Whippet does not understand what direction a sound is coming from. Be aware of your dog's needs, and, if necessary, teach him hand signals. There are some Whippets who are selectively deaf: they hear the sound of the food bowl – but not the call to go to bed!

Sight may fail in the last years, but it is amazing how well a dog can find his way around, providing you keep the furniture in the same place.

I feel that if your Whippet greets you with a wagging tail, eats his food with relish and is reasonably continent, he is still enjoying an acceptable quality of life. If you see any further deterioration – it is time to say goodbye.

Remember all the happy times you shared with your Whippet.

EUTHANASIA

When your Whippet is so old and frail, or so very ill, that life is no longer fun, you must be a responsible owner and make the decision to end his suffering.

Be guided by your vet and your own instincts, as to when it is time to let go. It is a very difficult time for both you and your companion. Do not be tempted to keep a Whippet going for your own sake. Think of the dog first; you must do what is right for him. Involve your family, and give them time to say goodbye to their friend. If you have children, explain what is happening, and why.

My vet has helped my dogs to go peacefully, and he always says that this is the last thing you can do for your dog. After all the love and affection they have given you and your family through their all-too-short lives, you must let them go with dignity.

If you can bear it, do stay with your dog to the last. He will feel secure with you there, holding him and talking to him. You may decide to ask your vet to come to your home if you feel it would be less upsetting for you and your Whippet.

There are pet crematoria; your vet will know the nearest and be able to advise you. Some of my Whippets have come home and are buried in the garden, some have been cremated – it all comes down to personal circumstances.

It is inevitable that you will grieve for your Whippet, but just remember that you did your best for him throughout his life. You gave him love and affection, and let him go at the right time.

6
The Versatile Whippet

The Whippet is fast, agile, elegant and intelligent – with that combination, it is not surprising that he can be trained to compete in a variety of canine disciplines.

RACING

Whippet racing is a traditional sport for the breed, and it has an enthusiastic following. The breed club in your area will have contacts for Whippet racing, and, to begin with, you can just go along and watch. If you decide you want to get involved in the sport, you can enrol as a club member.

Racing is held on Saturday or Sunday, depending on the club; in the summer there may be evening racing. Straight racing always takes place on a grass track, which is between 140 and 200 yards in length. The dogs run from wooden or metal traps which are either battery-operated, or hand-operated. They are similar to the traps used for Greyhound racing, but they are smaller in size.

The dogs chase a lure as opposed to the waved rag. Some are propelled by a bicycle frame, with the rear tyre removed to wind the cord round, but most clubs use a battery-operated car starter motor, which is mounted on a frame and fitted with a pulley. The speed is controlled by a circuit breaker. The lure itself is made of fleece or old fur coats.

GETTING STARTED

Whippets will naturally chase moving objects, a ball, a rubber ring or any toy you throw. If you decide to have a go at racing, take your puppy down to the track as early as possible to get him accustomed to the noise of the traps banging open and the dogs barking. He will soon get the hang of it all. Stand halfway up the track, well back, and let your puppy see the lure with the other

Give your Whippet plenty of encouragement when he first starts to chase the lure.

dogs in hot pursuit. It will not be long before your pup wants to have a go.

There are age limits as to how old your dog can be before he is allowed to chase a mechanical lure. In the UK, for example, the puppy must be at least six months old. When he is old enough, you can progress further with your training. Take him to the traps and show him the lure. Wave it in front of him and encourage him to have a go at tugging at it. Do this when there is a break in the racing, obviously making sure you have the trap operator's permission.

The next stage is to get the pup chasing the lure from halfway up the track. Get a friend to hand-slip your pup when you have walked about 20 yards away. Give the pup lots of praise when he chases the lure, and encourage him to grab the lure and worry it. Once he is running well, you can start introducing him to the open trap, and slip him through after the lure. Then you can have the trap closed in front, and just hold the dog in the trap, releasing him when the trap opens.

The next step is obvious: a closed trap, with the lure visible in front of it – just keep your fingers crossed that your Whippet will spring out and run!

TIME TO COMPETE

By the time your pup is 12 months old, the distance should

be gradually increased until he is running over 100 yards. While he is still running alone, get him used to wearing a muzzle. All Whippets race in muzzles, and so it is important that your pup is happy with it. Do not leave the muzzle on longer than needed, as it is not very comfortable and may put your dog off wearing it.

Once your Whippet is running confidently over 100 yards, and the racing manager gives the go-ahead, it is now time to let your Whippet run with other dogs. This is a most important test. It is important to choose a placid, honest dog to run with your pup. Give the pup a few yards start, and the more experienced dog will catch up and pass the pup. This will allow you to see if your pup has any vices as he is passed.

After three or four runs with one dog, your pup will be ready to run with three or more Whippets, and, hopefully, he will take it in his stride. Once your Whippet is running well with other dogs, he will need to run clearing trials. These are to pass him for racing in competition, and prove that he can run without interfering with the other dogs in a race.

If your Whippet qualifies, he will be entitled to a racing passport, which will carry his photo, details of his colour and markings, and the name of his sire and dam.

Most clubs do not encourage members to race their Whippets until they are 12 months old, as this gives them time to mature and finish growing.

Race meetings are friendly, family affairs. It is a great way to spend a day: running your Whippets, watching the younger dogs progress, and comparing last year's racers in the new season. It is fun for everyone – particularly the Whippets.

LURE COURSING

This is a relatively new sport, one that Whippets do really well at. In Britain, it is run by The British Sighthound Field Association, and is aimed at all the sighthound breeds. Meetings are held at different venues around the country from spring to autumn. Hounds always run against their own breed.

Before the meeting, the committee sets up the course. This is a continuous line, 500 metres long, run round bends and turns to imitate the line a hare would take. The meeting usually starts at

Lure coursing is well established in the USA, and is becoming increasingly popular in the UK.

9 am with the hounds being checked in with the secretary who allocates numbers. The owners are allowed to choose their partners or opponents, and they can decide whether to muzzle their dogs or not. The dogs do not have to run clearing trials as they do for racing, but the judge at a meeting can stop the proceedings if a dog is seen to be a danger to others.

There are two judges, and usually they own a different breed. They stand on a raised platform so that they can see the whole course. Each runner has a score sheet with 25 points for agility, 15 for enthusiasm, 15 for good follow, 20 for endurance, and 25 for speed. With so many different breeds competing, scoring is not all that easy.

The first two owners go to the start, where they hand their numbers to a runner who gives them to the judges. The 'Hunt Master' makes sure the lure operator and the judges are ready, and then asks the handlers if they are ready. This is the beginning of the course. As the lure goes past and ahead of the pair, he will shout "Tally-Ho" and on the "T" both dogs are slipped. Slipping early incurs a penalty.

The lure is usually one or two white plastic bags. These do not get waterlogged in wet grass, and they are light and easily replaced. It is amazing that Whippets will chase a plastic bag with just as much enthusiasm as they would a rabbit. Whippets can get burn marks from the line, and stop pads can also get skinned, but, on the whole, injuries do not happen very often.

This sport is not too

competitive, yet it offers a friendly match for you and your dog. Watching the dogs course is very exciting, as they can twist and turn so quickly. The course is usually turned about for the afternoon, so the dogs can have another go. The Whippets that do best are those that follow the lure and do not take short cuts. Some are so clever that they anticipate which way the lure will go after they have run the course once.

Before you go lure coursing, you must ensure your Whippet is fit enough. Do some road work to tone up the muscles and improve his stamina. If you are at all worried, take your dog to the vet for a check-up to make sure all is well – then go and enjoy yourselves.

COURSING

This is a very old sport with strict rules. It is the oldest field sport and evolved from man's use of dogs to hunt for food.

Coursing is run on a knockout principle. Almost all courses are

The judge, on horseback, waits for the slipper to release the first pair of Whippets.

made up of multiples of eight. Pairs of dogs run against each other, as drawn on the card, until there are only two dogs left for the final. In each course, the dog in the red collar is buckled on the slipper's left and the white collar on the right.

Whippet coursing is almost always walked, that is, members walk in a line with their dogs looking for hares, with the slipper with the two dogs in slips about 20 yards ahead, to the centre of the line. The slipper holds the two dogs to run on a quick-release slip lead, ready to slip them after the hare. The judge is mounted on a horse so that he can see what the dogs are doing. He follows them closely without interfering with the course, and awards points to each dog.

When a hare gets up, the slipper must make sure it is fit enough to be coursed, and he must make certain that both dogs have seen it. He will run forward until the hare is about 45 yards ahead, and then he will slip the dogs. The Whippets will race off, with the judge following at a gallop. The hare will twist and turn as it runs, and the dogs stay in pursuit until the hare escapes to cover. The judge will hold up a handkerchief showing the colour of the winning dog's collar.

Hare coursing is an emotive subject. It is important to understand that the object of the course is watching the dogs run, not killing the hare. It is a fact that 15 out of 16 hares will get away without the dogs getting near them.

Whippets are not bred solely for coursing, as they are for racing. Most come from show/coursing lines and have to stand 20 inches or lower at the shoulder. There are no weight groups as there are in racing.

AGILITY

More and more Whippets are having a go at Agility, with a considerable degree of success. Athletic and energetic, the Whippet soon learns the game.

To take part in Agility, a dog must be 12 months old, and should have a thorough grounding in basic obedience. Both dog and owner must be fit in order to run the course. There are clubs that specialise in Agility, and an instructor will help you to train your Whippet to negotiate all the different obstacles. He will have to learn to jump hurdles, go through tunnels, go up and down see-saws,

The energetic Whippet enjoys the thrills of Agility.

weave through bending poles, and climb up and down ramps at speed.

Do not attempt to rush your Whippet. It is important that he builds up confidence.

COMPETITIVE OBEDIENCE

Whippets who compete in Obedience are few and far between – this discipline does not come naturally to them. However, there is no reason why your Whippet should not reach a reasonable standard in Obedience training, and you can take part in the Canine Good Citizen Tests, which are open to all breeds.

The Good Citizen tests are aimed at making your canine companion a well-mannered dog. For example, he should be calm with strangers and allow himself to be handled, he should master basic obedience commands (e.g. walk well on the lead), and he

should be well behaved with other dogs. For more information, contact your national kennel club.

From there, you can progress to more formal Obedience training, if your dog shows a talent. There are hundreds of Obedience clubs, so you shouldn't have any difficulty finding one local to you. Whatever club you choose, do make sure they use only reward-based training – it is the only kind, effective way of teaching dogs.

There are many factors to Competitive Obedience, such as close heelwork, retrieving, distance control, nosework (identifying an article with a particular scent), and so on – plenty to keep a Whippet occupied!

THE SHOW DOG

Showing is a fascinating hobby, and is highly competitive when you reach Championship level. The sport is run by the national kennel club, and rules and regulations will vary depending on where you live.

In the UK, your puppy must be fully registered and six months old before you can enter a licensed show. There are strict rules that govern running any show; these are laid down by the Kennel Club to ensure that everything is run

Your Whippet will be judged against the criteria laid down in the Breed Standard.

correctly and safely for dogs, exhibitors and the public alike. Breaking the rules can result in any show society losing its licence, and exhibitors who break the regulations can be banned from taking part in activities run by the Kennel Club.

Showing is an ideal way of meeting people who are interested in the breed, and you can learn so much from the people who have been showing for a long time. The Whippet fraternity is always ready to welcome newcomers and to offer advice if asked.

IS MY DOG GOOD ENOUGH?

There is no point in getting involved with showing unless you have a dog that is worthy of being exhibited. Ask an experienced breeder to make an objective assessment of your dog. In order to be successful, he must conform as closely as possible to the criteria laid down in the Breed Standard, which is the written blueprint for the breed.

GENERAL APPEARANCE

The Whippet should present a combination of muscular power and strength, with elegance and a graceful outline.

HEAD

The head should be long and lean (think back to the Greyhound family), flat on top, and tapering to the muzzle with a slight stop. The jaws should be powerful and clean-cut, meeting in a perfect scissor bite. The nose should be

POINTS OF THE BREED STANDARD

The head should be long and lean; the eyes should be bright and alert.

The forelegs should be straight, with strong pasterns.

Correct angulation for the hindquarters.

The Whippet should have a long, effortless stride.

black; blue dogs may have a bluish nose, livers may have a nose of similar colour, and, in the parti-colour, a butterfly nose is permitted. The jaws should be strong with a perfect scissor bite.

BODY

The body must appear well balanced and in proportion.

- The neck should be long, muscular and elegantly arched.
- The shoulders should be oblique and muscular.
- The forelegs should be straight with strong pasterns, and the elbows set well under the body.
- The chest should be deep with good heart room. The back is broad with a slight rise over the loin (not a hump).
- The loin should be strong and the ribs well sprung.
- The hindquarters should be strong and broad across the thighs, with well-developed second thighs.
- The hocks should be well let down.
- The feet should be very neat with arched toes and thick, strong pads.
- The tail should be long and tapering. In action, it should be carried in a curve upwards, not gaily over the back.

MOVEMENT

When a Whippet moves, he should be true coming and going. He should show a long, effortless stride, with the front legs thrown well forward. He looks a bit like a racehorse, driving off well from its hind legs.

COAT

The coat should be fine, short and close in texture.

COLOUR

The Whippet can come in a great variety of colours, fawn, brindle, black, blue, white and parti-colour, or a mixture of the aforementioned.

SIZE

Height should be 47-51 cm (18.5 to 20 in) for a dog; 44-47 cm (17.5 to 18.5 in) for a bitch.

GETTING STARTED

Before you enter a show, you need to train your Whippet for the show ring. There are ringcraft classes that specialise in this discipline. There is usually a puppy section for beginners, but for the first week just sit and watch with your puppy. Let him get used to the other dogs and the noise. Training clubs are sociable places where you can converse and learn.

SHOW TRAINING

First, position the front legs.

Make sure your Whippet is standing straight behind.

The aim is to ensure your Whippet is shown to full advantage.

Practise moving your Whippet on a loose lead.

There should be an experienced handler to teach you how to stand your Whippet on the table, how to move him steadily up and down, and to circle round the ring with all the other dogs.

Your Whippet must learn to be examined by a stranger. This will involve having his teeth inspected, and a thorough examination of his body.

Shows are noisy places, and at some clubs they try to get the dogs ready for the show-ring atmosphere by giving a sudden burst of applause when the dogs are lined up.

When you feel confident that your Whippet is steady enough to enter a show, start with a small show. Whippets do not need lots of preparation to get them ready for a show; their short coats are easy to keep clean.

If you have a light-coloured dog, he may need a bath. Make sure you do this a couple of days before the show so that the coat has a chance to settle down. Check that the nails are short, the teeth are clean, and give the coat a good brush.

Finish by rubbing the coat with a silk scarf, velvet glove or chamois leather to bring out the shine.

AT THE SHOW

The equipment you will need when going to a show is:

- Your Whippet in tip-top condition
- A dog coat in case it is wet or cold
- A show lead (these are made of leather or nylon, and slip over the dog's head with a sliding band or clasp)
- A bristle brush

The judge will start by looking at all the entries in his class.

THE EXAMINATION

Each dog will be examined individually by the judge.

Here the judge is looking at the arch of the neck and the lay of the shoulder.

He moves on to look at the topline.

He now goes to the rear of the dog to look at the hindquarters and the tail-set.

The judge will find out more about the dog's conformation when he is moving.

- A grooming glove (rubber or fine bristle)
- A polishing-off cloth
- A bowl plus food and drinking water
- A towel
- A dog blanket
- A benching chain (in the UK, dogs are given their own benches)
- Wet-weather gear for you in case of bad weather
- Directions to the show ground.

Make sure you arrive in plenty of time to exercise your dog, give him a drink and settle him down. If you have a crate, your Whippet will be happy to settle in it. Check in the catalogue to ensure that your entry is correct, and check your ring number. Any mistakes should be reported to the show secretary at once. If all is in order and you have time, look around the show, relax and enjoy the day.

When it is time for your class, the ring steward will call out the class name and number. He will check each exhibit's ring number against the catalogue, marking those present and absent. You must display your ring number while in the ring. Once all the dogs are in the ring, the judge will expect all the exhibitors to pose

The judge must look at each entry and decide how closely the dog matches the Breed Standard.

their dogs, and then all the dogs will be asked to move around the ring once or twice.

After this, the judge will examine all the dogs individually on the table. He may ask how old your Whippet is – but do not address the judge unless he speaks to you first. You will be asked to move your dog straight across the ring, and then back to the judge. Try to walk in a straight line. Lots of exhibitors make the mistake of looking at the dog rather than at the judge, and end up in the wrong place. It is also important not to put yourself between your dog and the judge at any time. You may be asked to walk in a triangle, or continue round to the

end of the line. Some judges ask you not to pose your dog after moving, but to let him stand naturally. Practise this in training, as it is a very useful exercise.

After all the dogs in the class have been looked at, set your Whippet up as the last dog is going round. Keep your eye on the judge, since he might ask you to move your Whippet again. The class must now wait while the judge makes up his mind up. Keep talking to your Whippet, encouraging him to look alert if possible. The judge may pull out six or seven Whippets in no particular order, and send the rest out of the ring. He may then ask his short-listed dogs to move

Showing should always be fun – for both you and your dog.

again. He will then make his decision, and dogs will be placed from first to fourth (fifth at some shows).

Remember that this is a hobby and is supposed to be fun. It is a chance to meet friends and catch up on the news, so try not to get too tense. While in the ring, you can chat to your fellow exhibitors, and reassure your Whippet that he is doing fine and you are proud of him. If you do not get placed,

there is always another show and another judge. No dog will win all the time – not even the best.

This is a very basic outline of showing, but it will give you some idea of what to expect. I have made many friends over the years through my Whippets. However, our dogs are family pets first and foremost. Showing is a hobby we ask them to participate in – it should be a fun day out for them as much as it is for us.

7 *Health Care*

The vet will be an important person in your Whippet's life, so take the time to find a good veterinary practice that is knowledgeable about the breed. Check out the facilities, and the appointment system.

Veterinary care is expensive, so you may wish to consider taking out an insurance policy. Make sure you read the small print so you know what your Whippet is covered for. In the UK, the Blue Cross, the RSPCA and the PDSA run clinics for those who cannot pay, but they will ask for proof of entitlement to State benefits. Other countries have their own charity-based types of support.

PREVENTATIVE CARE

Routine preventative care will keep your Whippet in good health, and, if any problems arise, you will spot them at an early stage.

You are responsible for your Whippet's health from puppyhood to old age.

A syringe is used to give liquid worming medication.

INTERNAL PARASITES

Your puppy should have been wormed regularly in his first six months. The adult Whippet will need to be wormed at six-monthly intervals for both roundworm and tapeworm. It helps to note down on your calendar the dates that worming is due.

Medication for worming, in tablet or liquid form, can be obtained from your vet, who will advise you on dosage. Symptoms of worms include loss of condition, a poor coat, diarrhoea, loss of weight and anal itching, and dragging the bottom along the floor.

Hookworms and whipworms can cause anaemia and diarrhoea. Lungworm can cause the dog to cough while exercising. If you have any concerns, consult your vet.

EXTERNAL PARASITES

A Whippet may become infested with fleas, particularly if you also keep cats. I find that if my cats are kept clear of fleas, I have no problems with my Whippets. If your dog has fleas, they can be treated using a spot-on treatment, an insecticidal spray, or an insecticidal shampoo. Ask your vet for advice.

If you live in the country, your Whippet may pick up a tick. Ticks are blood-sucking; with powerful jaws, they attach themselves to the skin and dig in. A tick will suck its host's blood, gradually getting bigger, until it looks like a grey seed. At this point, the tick will drop off to digest its feed. It then awaits the next passing animal, and the cycle begins again.

When you remove a tick, it is very important to remove the whole tick, and not leave its mouthpiece embedded in the dog's skin. This can result in an abscess or an infection. I use alcohol (methylated spirits) to remove a tick. I wait until the tick dies, and then extract it carefully.

There are a number of

preparations that deal with both ticks and fleas. The spot-on treatments are easy to use and effective.

VACCINATIONS

It is essential that your Whippet is protected against the major contagious diseases (see Infectious Diseases, page 75).

A-Z OF COMMON AILMENTS

ALOPECIA

Also known as bald thigh syndrome. A few Whippets suffer from this; in dark colours it is more noticeable. Sometimes the cause is hormonal, and it has been found that some dogs receiving steroid or cortisone treatment may suffer from it.

Many Whippet owners have found that it is more apparent when a dog's pigmentation fades. The coat appears thin on the outer thighs due to the skin being paler.

Seek veterinary advice for a proper diagnosis.

ANAESTHETICS

If your Whippet needs a general anaesthetic, make sure that your vet is knowledgeable about the dosage required for the breed. A Whippet has no body fur, and the drug tends to stay in the body longer than in other breeds.

ANAL GLANDS

Whippets are not prone to having problems with their anal glands, which are situated on either side of the anus. The classic signs are bottom-shuffling on the ground, and chewing the area around the tail. Your vet can easily empty the glands, which will make the dog more comfortable.

CONSTIPATION

This can be caused by diet, so try changing your Whippet's diet, soak his feed and add some cooked green cabbage. Other causes of constipation are feeding bones; bone chips can compact in the colon causing hard faeces, which are difficult to pass. A dose of castor-oil will clear a blockage, if the dog is still having problems.

Sometimes a dog will suffer constipation because he is left indoors for too long, and does not wish to foul his surroundings. Dogs should be able to go outside at least every four hours. Travelling by car, or changing the feeding routine, can also lead to problems with constipation.

CYSTITIS

This condition affects bitches. The bitch will keep wanting to go outside and will squat as though urinating. You must take her to the vet as this is an inflammation of the urinary tract, usually caused by a bacterial infection. Your bitch

will soon recover and be back to normal with treatment.

Dogs can get a similar infection called balanitis. This is an infection of the penis and sheath. The discharge from the sheath will be the first thing you notice. The dog will have difficulty passing urine. You must visit the vet for this condition, as your dog will need antibiotics to clear it.

DIARRHOEA

This is passing frequent amounts of loose faeces. It is a common indication of many illnesses, some trivial but others possibly of a more serious nature. It is most usually caused by digestive problems, and the looseness will usually cease when the food causing it is withdrawn, or if a dietary change is made more slowly.

Treatment for diarrhoea is to starve the dog for 24 hours to allow the stomach and bowels to rest. Make sure water is always available. This should be boiled and then cooled. It is also a good idea to add a spoonful of glucose powder to the water.

When you recommence feeding, offer cooked eggs, chicken or fish with plain, boiled rice. Give small amounts at first, monitoring your Whippet's progress. Gradually increase the quantity until you feel your Whippet can go back to his usual diet.

If there is fresh blood in the faeces, contact your vet immediately, as it could mean Haemorraghic Gastroenteritis or Canine Parvovirus Infection, both serious diseases of the dog.

EAR INFECTIONS

Whippets suffer few ear problems as they have the type of ear where air can circulate freely. They can get canker, which is caused by ear mites. The inside of the ear will become red and hot, and there will be a smelly discharge. If the infection is severe, your Whippet will constantly scratch and shake his head. In all cases, you will need to consult your vet.

Your Whippet could also get a yeast infection, when a brownish, wet crust forms inside the ear. Again, you will need to see the vet as it is not possible to treat this yourself.

EPILEPSY

This can affect all breeds of dog and the fit, which is a convulsive seizure, usually occurs when the dog is relaxed or sleeping. It never occurs while the dog is active.

The first fit may occur between one and three years of age. A fit usually begins with a period of rigidity followed by shaking and muscular spasms, which progress to involuntary paddling with the

paws. This may only last for a minute or two, and the dog may recover quickly and appear perfectly normal. In other cases, the fit may go on longer; the dog takes longer to come out of it and may be disorientated for some hours afterwards. Make sure the dog cannot hurt himself during a fit, and avoid touching him. When your dog comes round, give reassurance.

Epilepsy can be controlled by medication so that your dog can achieve his full lifespan. Since fits can also be caused by brain tumours, previous traumas (such as a blow to the head), canine distemper, or liver disease, it is important to get an accurate diagnosis from your vet.

GASTRIC TORSION
This is not common in Whippets – it is more likely to affect Greyhounds. However, it is a life-threatening condition so it is important to recognise the signs

The stomach dilates and fills with gas and fluid. It then twists, causing a blockage. Symptoms are panting, attempts to vomit, restlessness and abdominal swelling. If this occurs, you must get your dog to the vet without delay.

Nobody really knows what causes this condition, which is also known as bloat. There is some evidence that it could result from feeding a large meal too soon after exercise.

HEAT STROKE
Whippets love to lie and sunbathe, or warm themselves by the fire. This is fine because you are on hand to keep an eye on your dog and ensure he does not become overheated. However, if you are

caught in a traffic jam in high temperatures, your Whippet may suffer from heat stroke.

You will need to cool your Whippet by any means available – cold water, ice, or even packets of frozen food. Do not cool the dog down too much – a 10-minute application should be sufficient. Then take your Whippet to the vet for a check-up.

If you are going on a long journey on a hot day, it is advisable to take a cool bag with ice packs in it. You can also soak a towel, put it in the freezer, and before you leave for your trip, put the towel in the cool bag.

INFECTIOUS DISEASES

There are a number of infectious diseases which affect dogs.

CANINE DISTEMPER

This is a virus infection with complications caused by a secondary bacterial invasion. It is transmitted from dog to dog by inhaling droplets from an infected animal. The incubation is around 7-21 days. If you suspect your Whippet has this disease, consult your vet immediately; it is highly infectious and can kill.

Your dog can be fully protected by vaccination, and then by keeping boosters up to date.

INFECTIOUS CANINE HEPATITIS

This is highly contagious, and has nothing to do with the human form of hepatitis. The incubation period is 5-7 days, and the dog may become ill very quickly. It is caught by swallowing material contaminated by saliva, urine or the faeces of infected dogs. Again, vaccination will give your dog full protection.

LEPTOSPIROSIS

There are two groups of this bacteria that can affect dogs: Leptospira icterohaemorrhagiae and Leptospira canicola. Both of these can be passed on to children and adults, and are notifiable diseases. The incubation period is 5-15 days. The bacteria are carried by rats, and transmitted to dogs which kill rats, or via rat urine. The symptoms are a high temperature and great thirst, abdominal pain, coated tongue, diarrhoea containing blood, jaundice and persistent vomiting. This disease is also covered by vaccination. It is very important to keep boosters up to date.

Leptospira Canicola symptoms are very similar to L. Icterohaemorrhagiae, but less marked. This infection can cause damage to the kidneys which may become critical in later life. It should be remembered that this infection can be passed on to man.

CANINE PARVOVIRUS INFECTION (CPV)

This is a very tough and persistent virus, recognised in dogs since 1978. The incubation period is five days. It is transmitted from dog to dog via a virus excreted in the faeces, via human clothing, footwear and objects that may have been contaminated by an infected dog. The virus can remain viable for up to a year.

It can affect dogs from four weeks old to old age, but it is most severe in the first year when it can be fatal. The symptoms are depression, severe vomiting, abdominal pain, refusal of food and water, plus very bad diarrhoea, often with blood. If the dog is going to survive, he will be noticeably better within four to five days of the onset of the illness. You will need to seek urgent veterinary attention.

Your puppy will be vaccinated against this disease, and you will need to continue with boosters.

INFECTIOUS CANINE TRACHEOBRONCHITIS (KENNEL COUGH)

This disease is transmitted from dog to dog where there is a large gathering in a show environment or in kennels. A dog becomes infected inhaling airborne virus particles that have been exhaled by infected dogs. The worst time of year for kennel cough is summer when dogs go into kennels and there are lots of shows.

The symptoms are a harsh cough; white froth may be coughed up as well. Most dogs continue behaving normally, and the infection runs its course. If a dog is more severely affected, he will need treatment from the vet.

This can be a long-lasting disease, but it is seldom life-threatening (with the exception of very young puppies). A vaccination can be given, and this will be required if your dog is going into boarding kennels.

PYOMETRA

This is a very serious problem for bitches, in which the uterus fills up with pus. There are two forms. Open pyometra will cause a high temperature and an increased thirst, plus a thick, brownish, smelly discharge from the vagina. Closed pyometra is much worse as the pus does not discharge. Instead, it seeps through the walls of the uterus and poisons the bloodstream. Both types are life-

threatening, and you must contact your vet quickly.

RHINITIS

This is an inflammation of the nasal cavities. The signs are an excessive mucky discharge from the nostrils. Remove any discharge with moist cotton wool, and, if you find pus in it, contact your vet. This can be a difficult condition to cure. Your Whippet may have a foreign body up his nose, so it is essential to get the correct diagnosis.

SKIN CONDITIONS

There are a number of skins problems that can affect Whippets. **Flea allergy:** If a Whippet has sensitive skin, he may suffer from a flea allergy. This will make the dog uncomfortable and itchy, and he will bite and scratch, making his skin sore. To prevent this,

follow a strict de-fleaing routine.
Mange: This is a nasty skin condition, but the new treatments are usually very successful. Mange is caused by the mange mite burrowing under the dog's skin. The condition is transferred from dog to dog. If you live in the country, foxes can be carriers. It is important to get this condition diagnosed and treated. You must also wash all bedding and clean the dog's environment. Mange can also be caught by humans and causes an irritating rash on the hands and wrists, and any part of the body that has had close contact with the infected dog.
Ringworm: This is a fungal, non-irritating condition that causes bald patches, which are usually ring-shaped. Diagnosis is by laboratory testing. It is important to get a correct diagnosis as humans can catch ringworm.

Scurfy coat: Sometimes your Whippet's skin may be scurfy. The best course of action is to use a good-quality dog shampoo designed for this problem. Check that the diet you are feeding has enough oil in it, and groom regularly. This will stimulate the skin and help to slough off the dry particles. Evening primrose oil is also beneficial.

UNDESCENDED TESTICLES

Sometimes a dog will retain one or both testicles. In most cases, a Whippet puppy will have both testicles visible at four to eight weeks old. A retained testicle can result in a tumour, so you will need to consult your vet, who will probably recommend castration.

VOMITING

Dogs are perfect vomiting machines – anything your Whippet swallows that does not agree with him will usually return very quickly. If dogs eat too quickly, they can bring up their dinner almost as fast as it goes down. Dogs who do this are probably better fed alone to avoid gulping food.

Prolonged vomiting will need to be investigated, as your Whippet will very quickly become dehydrated through loss of fluid. Dehydration can be recognised by picking up a fold of skin on the dog's back – it should spring straight back. If it remains sticking up, the dog is dehydrated and will need treatment. Small sips of water, with a little glucose, will help keep the energy levels up until you can get to the vet.

Regurgitation is a more passive type of vomiting. Some dogs will eat their food then sneak off and regurgitate it, and eat it more slowly away from disturbances. It is quite normal for bitches to regurgitate their own partially digested food when they are weaning puppies.

Retching is usually caused by an obstruction in the mouth or throat, or the result of a sore throat and cough. You should check with your vet if this persists.

Vomiting associated with disease such as pyometra, CPV, kidney disease and gastroenteritis is usually accompanied by loss of appetite, depression and diarrhoea. Seek veterinary help at once, especially if there is blood in the vomit.

A blockage in the digestive tract will also cause vomiting. If you suspect your Whippet has swallowed something and it has

With good care and management, your Whippet should live a long and healthy life.

become stuck, go to the vet without delay.

If you know your Whippet has eaten poison, such as slug bait or mouse poison, seek urgent veterinary attention. It will help if you take a sample of the poison and the package with you, as this will help the vet to treat your dog.

SUMMARY

We are lucky that the Whippet is generally a hardy breed that suffers few serious health problems. If you feed a well-balanced diet, give the correct exercise, and follow a programme of preventative health care, your Whippet should live a long and happy life.